MYSTERY HUNTERS

BIGFOOT
AND OTHER MONSTERS

By John Hawkins

PowerKiDS
press.
New York

Published in 2012 by The Rosen Publishing Group, Inc.
29 East 21st Street, New York, NY 10010

Copyright © 2012 Arcturus Publishing Limited

Author: John Hawkins
Editor and Picture Researcher: Joe Harris
U.S. Editor: Kara Murray
Design: Emma Randall
Cover Design: Emma Randall

Picture credits:
Corbis: 15, 22, 24. Cryptomundo.com: 7. Idaho State University: 8. iStockphoto: 27. Mary Evans Picture Library: 14. Science Photo Library: Cover. Shutterstock: 1, 5, 6, 16, 17, 18, 20, 25, 26, 28, 29. TopFoto: 9, 11, 12. Wikimedia: 10, 19. William Stoneham: 4, 13.

Library of Congress Cataloging-in-Publication Data

Hawkins, John.
 Bigfoot and other monsters / by John Hawkins.
     p. cm. — (Mystery hunters)
 Includes index.
 ISBN 978-1-4488-6431-7 (library binding) — ISBN 978-1-4488-6445-4 (pbk.) — ISBN 978-1-4488-6446-1 (6-pack)
 1. Sasquatch—Juvenile literature. 2. Monsters—Juvenile literature. I. Title.
 QL89.2.S2H39 2012
 001.944—dc23

                                    2011026817

Printed in China
SL002063US

CPSIA Compliance Information: Batch #AW2102PK: For Further Information contact Rosen Publishing, New York, New York at 1-800-237-9932

CONTENTS

BIGFOOT: FIRST IMPRESSIONS

The native peoples of North America are the source of the oldest stories about Bigfoot, or Sasquatch. Different tribes have different names for it. They called it *chenoo* or *kiwakwe*. They all describe a creature covered in fur that looks like a large human and lives in remote forested areas.

WILD MAN OF THE WOODS

As early as 1793, European settlers in North America were reporting sightings of a "hairy ape man." A legend soon grew up of a "wild man of the woods." There were several newspaper reports of scary encounters where hunters and trappers stumbled across ape-men during the nineteenth and early twentieth centuries.

▼ Ape-men have been sighted in many different countries, and have been given many different names. Could they in fact belong to the same species?

Yowie

Yeren

Maricoxi

Orange Pendak

Yeti

Wildman

▲ Could the forests around Mount St. Helens be home to the Sasquatch?

STOLEN AWAY

During that same summer of 1924, a Canadian, Albert Ostman, claimed he was seized by Sasquatches. He was camping in the mountains of British Columbia, when one night he was carried away in his sleeping bag by four hairy, apelike people. For several days they did not allow him to escape. Eventually, he managed to get away by distracting them with his snuffbox.

BATTLE OF APE CANYON

In July 1924, an Oregon newspaper ran a story about a group of gold prospectors in the Mount St. Helens region who came under attack from a group of Sasquatches. According to their account, they first saw a creature while getting water. It was over 6.5 feet (2 m) tall and was watching them from behind a tree. That night, three Sasquatches attacked the men's cabin. They pounded the walls with large rocks. Two creatures climbed on the roof. However, by the next morning, the creatures had gone.

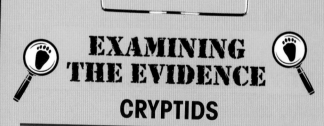

EXAMINING THE EVIDENCE
CRYPTIDS

The creatures described in this book are all legendary creatures, or cryptids. Do they actually exist? It's certainly true that many people claim to have seen them. However scientists argue that eyewitness reports are not enough evidence to prove a creature exists. Witnesses might mistake a sighting of one creature for something else or be the victims of hoaxes.

BIGFOOT: THE SIGHTINGS CONTINUE

Four years after Albert Ostman's encounter, another man claimed to have been carried away in the night. Muchalat Harry was a fur trapper from Vancouver Island, in British Columbia, who said he was taken from his camp and captured by around 20 Sasquatches. Seeing a pile of gnawed bones nearby, he became terrified that he would be eaten. Like Ostman, he escaped to tell his tale.

▲ *Bigfoot is often described as a giant hairy man.*

RUBY CREEK INCIDENT

George and Jennie Chapman and their three children lived near the village of Ruby Creek, British Columbia. During the summer of 1941, while George was away working, Jennie and her eldest son claimed to have spotted a gigantic hairy man near their house. He cried out and began striding towards them. Alarmed, they fled. Jennie shepherded her children out of the house under a blanket, hoping the Sasquatch wouldn't see them.

▲ *This photograph of "Bigfoot" was taken by a backpacker on November 17, 2005.*

THE FAMILY VANISHED

When George arrived home two hours later, he found the door to the outhouse smashed in, food scattered around and half eaten, and giant footprints in the soil. It was with relief that he found his family safe at Jennie's father's house.

On five more nights after that, the family heard the cry of the Sasquatch and found footprints not far from their house.

STRANGE STORIES

William Roe's account

Roe was a hunter and trapper living in Alberta, Canada. One day in October 1955, he was approaching an old, abandoned mine in Tête Jaune Cache when he saw what he took to be a grizzly bear in the bushes. When the creature emerged into the clearing, he saw it wasn't a bear. It looked more like a giant hairy man. It squatted down and began eating leaves off a bush. Then it caught his scent and looked at him. Standing up, it walked away rapidly. Roe raised his rifle to shoot, but then the creature glanced back and Roe said he saw a spark of humanity in its eyes. Suddenly he felt that killing this creature would be murder, so he let it go.

BIGFOOT: HITTING THE HEADLINES

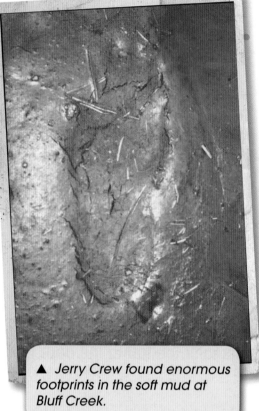

▲ *Jerry Crew found enormous footprints in the soft mud at Bluff Creek.*

Modern interest in Bigfoot began in 1958, sparked by events at Bluff Creek in Northern California. On the morning of August 27, a construction crew building a road through this area turned up for work to discover some strange footprints in the soil. They were described as looking like naked human footprints. However they were different in one crucial way: they were much bigger.

FOOTPRINTS

The man who discovered the prints was bulldozer operator Jerry Crew. When more prints appeared on October 1, he made a plaster of paris cast of one of them and was photographed with it for the local newspaper. The story was taken up by newspapers across the United States and the world.

Several cryptozoologists (people who study cryptids) visited the site and made more footprint casts, as well as collecting eyewitness reports of encounters. Later, it emerged that the head of the construction firm, Ray Wallace, owned a pair of gigantic wooden feet. He had faked many of the Bigfoot prints. However whether he faked them all is open to debate.

▲ *This photographer is measuring a Bluff Creek footprint before taking a picture.*

In 1961, Larry Martin claimed he was chased by a Sasquatch in the hills above Alpine, Oregon. In June 1963, Stan Mattson reported witnessing a female Sasquatch with a baby catching small fish near Yale, in Washington State. And in October 1966, the Corey family reported a visit by a 7-foot (2 m)- tall Sasquatch, which, they said, killed the family dog.

THE REPORTS MULTIPLY

After the Bluff Creek episode, stories of Bigfoot encounters came flooding in. In the summer of 1959, a woman named Mrs. Bellevue was startled by a humanlike ape watching her from behind some trees while she was camping in British Columbia.

EXAMINING THE EVIDENCE

DID RAY WALLACE FAKE ALL THE BLUFF CREEK FOOTPRINTS?

Skeptics believe that practical joker Wallace was responsible for all the footprints found at Bluff Creek, including the original ones found by Jerry Crew. They say that Wallace's company was falling behind with its work and Wallace wanted to come up with a reason to extend the deadline. On the other hand, Wallace was away from the state on business when at least some of the tracks appeared. Believers in the Sasquatch argue that Wallace took to his hoaxing after the first prints appeared in Bluff Creek, so that he could exploit them.

BIGFOOT: FILMING A SASQUATCH

On October 20, 1967, Roger Patterson shot a short film of a mysterious creature in Bluff Creek, in Northern California. This is the most important single piece of evidence for the existence of Bigfoot. Patterson and his companion Bob Gimlin have been called heroes by some but described by others as frauds or victims of a hoax.

▲ *This famous image from the Patterson film shows the Bigfoot glancing behind it.*

PATTERSON'S STORY

Patterson and Gimlin were both part-time rodeo riders. They headed into the wilderness that October with a camera in search of Sasquatch. They had been riding for some hours, apparently, when they reached a creek running through a canyon. Beside the creek, about 25 feet (8 m) from them, they saw a creature. It also spotted them and began walking away. Patterson grabbed the camera and ran after the Sasquatch. He tripped and fell at one point but kept filming. The creature turned to look at him as it walked. Soon it passed around a bend and out of sight.

OTHER EVIDENCE

Since 1967, other Sasquatch films have come to light. However none footage (1995), filmed on a rainy night in Northern California, shows a similar-looking creature moving in the beam of a car's headlights. The Manitoba footage (2005), shot on the banks of the Nelson River, in Manitoba, shows a strange figure on the opposite bank. It is too far away to be sure what it is, though.

▲ Roger Freeman with his casts of "Bigfoot prints." He found so many prints that some of his colleagues became suspicious.

of these match the quality of the original Patterson film. They include the Freeman footage, shot in 1994 by forestry worker Paul Freeman near Walla Walla, Washington State. It shows a hairy humanlike figure crossing a path and then disappearing into the woods. The Redwoods

 EXAMINING THE EVIDENCE

WHAT DOES THE PATTERSON FILM SHOW?

Bigfoot researchers who have studied the film suggest it is a female Bigfoot, as two mammary glands are visible on its front. Some people have questioned the film's authenticity. They say that if the film is played at a slightly faster speed, it looks like a human in a costume. However, some elements of the film do make scientific sense. For example, biologists have said that for such a creature to walk upright, it would need an extended heel. The creature in the film has an extended heel. Film industry experts have said the film was not made using special effects.

THE SKUNK APE

In the mid-1960s, Florida police received several reports claiming that an apelike creature was living in the state's swamplands. It sounded similar to Bigfoot, except for one thing. It smelled like a mixture of rotten eggs and manure. One witness said it had the scent of a skunk rolling around in a garbage truck. It soon became known as the Skunk Ape.

▼ *This photograph allegedly shows a Florida Skunk Ape.*

▲ *An artist's impression of Jennifer Ward's encounter with a Skunk Ape*

FOUL ODOR

In 1966, Eula Lewis of Brooksville, Florida, reported being chased into her house by an apelike creature with a round head and long arms. In July of the same year, Ralph Chambers spotted what he called a hairy man moving through forests bordering the Anclote River in Florida. He said it had a rancid, putrid odor. Reports of the Skunk Ape continued to flow in, and in August 1971, Henry Ring, a Broward County rabies control officer, was sent out to investigate. He found no apes but did discover some strange apelike tracks.

The sightings continued to be reported through the 1980s and 1990s. In 2000, a group of tourists in the Everglades saw a large, apelike animal moving around in a swamp. Later it was seen crossing the road outside the house of a local fire chief. One man took a photograph of the beast as it retreated into swampland.

STRANGE STORIES
Creature in the cellar

In August 1979, a team of workmen was sent to demolish a remote farmstead near Oxhopee, Florida. They noticed a foul smell coming from the cellar and assumed an animal had died in there. Two hours later, one of the men saw a creature climb out of the cellar. The man yelled and the other men came running. They saw the creature walk upright across open ground before disappearing into some trees. It was about 5 feet (1.5 m) tall and covered in reddish hair.

THE YETI

In 1921, a team of British mountaineers scaling the north face of Mount Everest, noticed dark shapes moving in the snow above them. When they reached the site, they found large, humanlike footprints. Their Sherpa guides called the creature *metoh-kangmi*, which translates as "abominable snowman." The other name for it is the yeti.

▲ *The photograph that sparked international interest in the yeti*

FOOTPRINTS IN THE SNOW

Four years later, N. A. Tombazi, a Greek photographer, was on an expedition in the Himalayas when he and his guides caught sight of a humanlike figure in the distance. The creature soon departed but again left strange footprints in the snow. Footprints that may have belonged to a yeti were also found on Everest by mountaineers Eric Shipton and Michael Ward in 1951. They were seen again by Sir Edmund Hilary and Sherpa Tenzing Norgay on their celebrated climb to the summit of that mountain in 1953.

A TAILLESS ANIMAL

Over the years, further encounters have been reported. In 1974, a Sherpa girl and her yaks were apparently attacked by a yeti. In 1976, a report told of how six forestry workers came across a strange, tailless animal covered in reddish-brown fur. Some hair samples were obtained to back up these reports. The hairs were studied but could not be identified.

In 1986, British physicist Tony Woodbridge spotted what he believed to be a large, hairy, powerfully built creature about 500 feet (150 m) away. However, closer examination of the photographs he took convinced Woodbridge it had been a tree stump.

▲ Could the yeti be an ape that has adapted to cold climates?

EYEWITNESS TO MYSTERY
HAIRY MAN

Pang Gensheng, a farmer from in Shaanxi in China, describes an encounter with a yeti: "In the summer of 1977 I went to Dadi Valley to cut logs. Between 11 a.m. and noon I ran into the 'hairy man' in the woods. It came closer and I got scared so I retreated until my back was against a stone cliff.... I raised my ax, ready to fight for my life. We stood like that, neither of us moving for a long time. Then I groped for a stone and threw it at him. It hit his chest. He uttered several howls and rubbed the spot.... Then he turned ... and leaned against a tree, then walked away...."

THE BIG GRAY MAN

It is said that on the mountain of Ben MacDhui, in the Scottish Highlands, there lurks a huge and terrifying creature. They call it Am Fear Liath Mor, or the Big Gray Man. Some see it as an old figure in robes, a giant, or even a devil. The creature, so they say, is physically threatening and causes terrifying panic in those who come near it. Scientists have suggested that the creature may be a result of hallucinations caused by isolation or exhaustion.

▼ Some believe that strange creatures roam the slopes of Ben MacDhui.

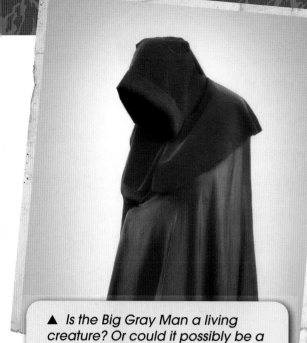

▲ *Is the Big Gray Man a living creature? Or could it possibly be a supernatural apparition?*

FOOTSTEPS

In 1891, Norman Collie, an experienced climber, was descending through mist from the peak of Ben MacDhui when he heard footsteps behind him. At first, he assumed it was an echo of his own footfalls. But the noises did not match his movements. It sounded like a giant was following him. Terrified, he ran blindly for around 5 miles (8 km) down the mountain until he could no longer hear the noise.

FOREST CHASE

In the early 1990s, three men were walking in a forest close to the mountain when they spotted a humanlike figure running across the track a little way ahead of them. A few weeks later, the men were driving in the area when they realized they were being followed by the same being. The creature kept pace with the car, even at speeds of 45 miles per hour (72 km/h), before eventually disappearing.

? FACT HUNTER

BROCKEN SPECTERS

What are they? Optical illusions that can be seen on misty mountainsides or cloud banks when the Sun is low. The observer's shadow is cast onto low-lying clouds opposite the Sun.

What visual effect do they cause? They create the illusion of a large, shadowy humanoid figure.

Why does the figure appear so large? The magnification of size is an optical illusion that happens when the observer thinks his shadow is at the same distance as faraway land objects seen through gaps in the clouds.

THE LOCH NESS MONSTER

Of all the world's mythical beasts, perhaps the most famous is Nessie, the Loch Ness monster. Loch Ness is a freshwater lake in the Scottish Highlands, 24 miles (38 km) long and up to 1,000 feet (304 m) deep. Although stories of a creature in the loch have been told ever since 565 AD when Saint Columba was said to have seen one, it wasn't until the twentieth century that the phenomenon really took off.

EARLY SIGHTINGS

In April 1933, a local couple spotted an enormous animal rolling and playing in the water. Soon afterwards, a fisherman saw it, describing it as having a long neck, a serpentine head, and a huge hump. He believed it to be around 30 feet (9 m) in length. In July of that year, a family from London almost crashed into a massive, dark, long-necked animal that strolled across their path and then disappeared into the water.

▼ Urquhart Castle overlooks Loch Ness.

▲ The famous "surgeon's photograph."

FAMOUS PHOTO

Over the years, there have been many attempts to capture Nessie on film. One of the most famous photographs, showing the monster's head and neck, was published in 1934. The "surgeon's photograph," as it became known, was later revealed to be a fake. Meanwhile, the sightings continued. In June 1993, a couple was on the bank of the loch when they saw a huge creature rolling around in the water. They estimated it to be over 40 feet (12 m) long, with a giraffelike neck.

SEARCHING FOR NESSIE

There have been about 3,000 similar sightings by individuals. The Academy of Applied Science in Boston, Massachusetts, launched the first scientific expedition in the early 1970s. Using underwater cameras, the project captured images of what looked like a an 8-foot (2.4 m)- long flipper and an unusual 20-foot (6 m)- long body. However, a later expedition revealed the image to be a tree stump.

EYEWITNESS TO MYSTERY

NECK LIKE A CONGER EEL

In early May 2001, at around 6 a.m., James Gray and Peter Levings were fishing on Loch Ness, when Gray spotted a movement 460 feet (140 m) away and saw something sticking out of the water. Then the object began to rise: "Soon, it was about 6 feet (1.8 m) out of the water but seconds later it had become a black kind of blob as it disappeared. It had curled forward and gone down.... This was certainly no seal. It had a long black neck almost like a conger eel, but I couldn't see a head. It didn't seem to bend very much but as it went under it sort of arched and disappeared."

NESSIE: THE HUNT CONTINUES

The search for the Loch Ness monster continues to this day. In 1987, scientists carried out Operation Deepscan, an organized, structured sonar sweep of the loch. Deepscan didn't find the monster, but it did report various hard-to-explain sonar echoes moving around in the extreme depths of the loch.

STRANGE NOISES

In March 2000, a team of Norwegian scientists picked up bizarre grunting and snorting noises in the loch's water. They sounded very similar to noises recorded in a Norwegian lake that also has a monster legend attached to it.

▲ Could the Loch Ness monster be a survivor from the age of the dinosaurs? This digital image shows a plesiosaur called Elasmosaurus.

NESSIE'S LAIR

Recent sonar explorations have revealed huge underwater caverns near the bottom of Loch Ness. These have been nicknamed Nessie's Lair. Some scientists suggest they may be big enough to hide a family of creatures. If the monster does exist, a breeding colony would be needed for its survival.

COULD NESSIE BE A PLESIOSAUR?

Experts have suggested that Nessie seems to bear a strong resemblance to a creature now thought to be extinct: the plesiosaur, a marine reptile not found on Earth for over 60 million years. Plesiosaurs had large flippers, a small head, and a large body. Sometimes they are described as "snakes threaded through the bodies of turtles." Some cryptozoologists believe that a few of these animals may have been stranded in the loch after the Ice Age. But as a marine reptile, the plesiosaur was probably cold-blooded. So it would be unlikely to survive the chilly conditions of a Scottish lake.

? FACT HUNTER

LAKE MONSTER

What is it? A lake monster is a freshwater-dwelling, large animal that is the subject of mythology, rumor, or local folklore but whose existence lacks scientific support. Nessie is one of the most famous lake monsters.

Do they really exist? Most scientists believe lake monsters to be exaggerations of misinterpretations of known and natural phenomena or else fabrications and hoaxes. They may be seals, otters, deer, diving water birds, large fish, logs, mirages, or unusual wave patterns.

What other lake monsters are there? Examples include the Thetis Lake monster (Thetis Lake, British Columbia, Canada), Bessie (Lake Erie, Ohio), Auli (Lake Chad, Chad), and Brosno Dragon (Brosno Lake, Russia).

THE LUSCA

Around the Bahamas and the southeastern coast of the United States there are tales of a giant octopus that captures unwary swimmers and small boats. The people of the islands call it the Lusca and believe it lives in deep underwater caves.

MYSTERIOUS CARCASS

One evening in November 1896, two men were cycling along the coast just outside the town of St. Augustine, Florida, when they spotted a huge, silvery pink carcass on the beach. It was 23 feet (7 m) long, 18 feet (5.5 m) wide, and seemed to have multiple legs. It weighed 7 to 8 tons (6–7 t). The men informed Dr. Dewitt Webb, a local scientist, who came to examine the corpse. Webb was convinced it was some kind of octopus.

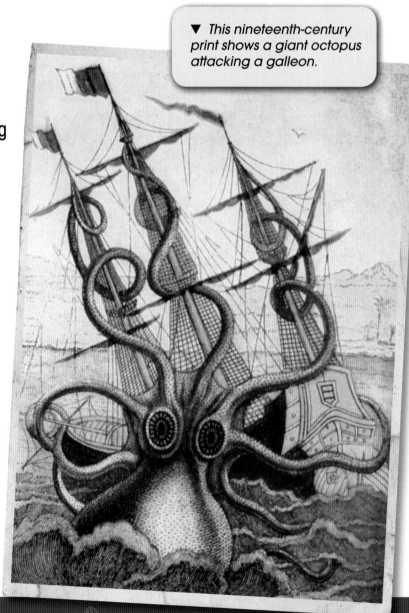

▼ *This nineteenth-century print shows a giant octopus attacking a galleon.*

However, other experts disagreed, saying it was probably just the head of a sperm whale. Further tests on samples from the corpse, carried out in 1971 and 1986, seemed to confirm that it was indeed part of a gigantic octopus. But even more detailed tests in 1995 suggested the carcass was actually part of a whale.

GIANT OCTOPUS

Locals say the Lusca can grow to over 75 feet (23 m) long and some say up to 200 feet (60 m). No octopus approaching that size has ever been found. However, on January 18, 2011, the body of what appeared to be a giant octopus washed ashore on Grand Bahama Island, in the Bahamas. According to eyewitness reports, the remains represented only a portion of the head and mouthparts of the original creature. Local fishermen estimate the total length of the creature to have been 20 to 30 feet (6–9 m).

RECORD BREAKER

Scientists suggest that the Lusca may, in fact, be a giant squid, which has been known to grow to very large sizes. The largest squid on record was a female giant squid that washed ashore on a New Zealand beach in 1887. It was 59 feet (18 m) long and weighed 1 ton (1 t).

STRANGE STORIES
The Chickcharney
The Lusca is not the only cryptid that haunts the Bahamas. The Chickcharney is a creature resembling an owl that reportedly lives in the forests of Andros Island. According to legend, it is about 3 feet (1 m) tall, furry, feathered, and ugly. Travelers who meet the Chickcharney and treat it well are rewarded with good luck. Those who don't will be the victim of hard times.

THE MONGOLIAN DEATH WORM

Under the burning sand dunes of the Gobi Desert there is said to lurk a creature so feared by the Mongolian people, they are scared even to speak its name. When they do, they call it the *allghoi khorkhoi*, or "large intestine worm," because this fat, red, deadly snakelike monster looks similar to a cow's intestines. In the West, the monster has come to be known as the Mongolian death worm.

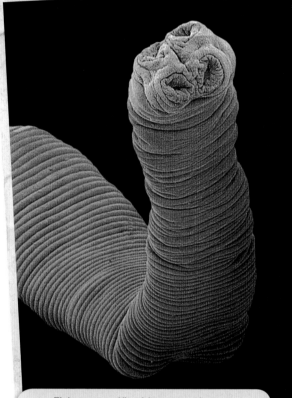

▲ *This magnified image shows a parasitic tapeworm, which lives in the human gut. Could the Mongolian death worm be related to this real-life monster?*

DEATH FROM A DISTANCE

According to legend, this giant worm, measuring up to 5 feet (1.5 m) in length, can kill people instantly. Some believe it spits a lethal toxin. Others say it emits a massive electrical charge. However it kills, it does so quickly and can do it from a distance.

Mongolian nomads believe the giant worm covers its prey with an acidic substance that turns everything it touches yellow and corroded. Legend says that as the creature begins to attack, it raises half its body out of the sand and starts to inflate until it

▲ *The death worm is described as looking similar to a swollen intestine.*

creature's existence. One man, Ivan Mackerle, carried out many interviews and came to the conclusion that the death worm was more than just a legend. However, no one can say for sure what it is. Experts are certain it is not a real worm because the Gobi Desert is too hot an area for annelids to survive. Some suggest it may be a skink. However, skinks have little legs and scaly skin, while eyewitnesses insist the worm is limbless and smooth bodied. The most probable explanation is that the death worm is a type of venomous snake.

explodes, releasing the lethal poison over the unfortunate victim. The poison is so powerful, the prey dies instantly.

WHAT IS IT?

In recent years, Western investigators have searched for evidence of the

STRANGE STORIES
The Minhocão

Another legendary wormlike creature is the Minhocão, of southern Brazil. This giant creature allegedly lives at the fords of rivers, where witnesses have claimed to see it drag livestock under the water. According to an account written in 1877, the Minhocão can dig trenches big enough to divert rivers or overturn trees. It is said to have scaly black skin "as thick as pine tree bark," a piglike snout, and two tentacle-like structures protruding from its head.

MOTHMAN

In early November 1966, various sightings of a huge, strange "bird" were reported around Point Pleasant, West Virginia. On November 12, five gravediggers preparing a plot claimed they saw a "brown human being" take to the air from some nearby trees and pass over their heads. The creature came to be known as Mothman.

FLYING MONSTER

On November 15, two young couples were driving together in an area just outside Point Pleasant. As they passed an old generator plant, they noticed that its door appeared to have been ripped off. They then claimed to see two red eyes shining out of the gloom at them. The eyes belonged to a creature shaped like a man but

▲ What was the Mothman? We may never know.

▲ *According to witnesses, the Mothman had glowing red eyes.*

the vehicle reaching high speed. The creature disappeared before they reached Point Pleasant.

BRIDGE DISASTER

In the year that followed, Mothman was seen by many witnesses, including firemen and pilots. Then, on December 15, 1967, the Silver Bridge linking Point Pleasant to Ohio suddenly collapsed, causing the death of 46 people. Mothman was rarely seen after that. Some people believe the bridge disaster may have been the monster's terrible final act.

more than 7 feet (2 m) tall, with wings folded against its back. As the creature approached, the young people ran away. Glancing behind, they saw it take to the air, rising straight up without flapping its wings. It had a 10-foot (3 m) wingspan and kept pace with their car despite

EYEWITNESS TO MYSTERY
TERRIBLE GLOWING EYES

On November 16, 1966, a young mother reported a scary incident. She said she was driving to a friend's house just outside Point Pleasant when she saw a strange red light in the sky. Arriving at her destination, she heard something rustling near her car. She recalled, "It rose up slowly from the ground. A big gray thing. Bigger than a man, with terrible, glowing eyes." As she fled into the house with her small daughter, the creature followed and stared in through the windows. The police were called, but by the time they arrived, the creature had disappeared.

THE OGOPOGO

Okanagan Lake is in British Columbia, Canada. It is around 100 miles (160 km) long and up to 984 feet (300 m) deep. The native Salish tribe believed in a terrible serpent, which they called N'ha-a-itk, or the "Lake Demon." They said the beast had a cave dwelling near the middle of the lake, and they would make sacrifices to please the monster.

THE MODERN LEGEND

European settlers initially scoffed at the legends. However, over the years the Ogopogo, as it came to be known, has established itself in the minds of many who live nearby. European immigrants started seeing strange phenomena in the lake during the mid-1800s. One of the first stories told of a man crossing the lake with his two tethered horses swimming behind. Some strange force pulled the animals

▼ Okanagan Lake

▲ *The Ogopogo seems like a more aggressive cousin of the Loch Ness monster.*

MOVIE MONSTER

The Ogopogo was allegedly filmed in 1968. The film shows a dark object propelling itself through shallow water near the shore. Another film, in 1989, showed a snakelike animal flicking its tail. Between August 2000 and September 2001, three local companies offered a $2 million reward to anyone who could find proof that the fabled Ogopogo existed.

under, and the man saved himself by cutting the horses loose.

SIGHTINGS

Most alleged sightings have occurred around the city of Kelowna, near the center of the lake. Witnesses say the creature is up to 50 feet (15 m) long, with green skin, several humps, and a huge, horselike head. A major sighting was in 1926 when the occupants of 30 cars at Okanagan Mission Beach supposedly saw the monster.

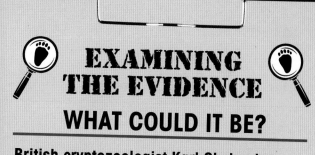

EXAMINING THE EVIDENCE
WHAT COULD IT BE?

British cryptozoologist Karl Shuker has categorized the Ogopogo as a "many hump" variety of lake monster. He has suggested it could be a kind of primitive serpentine whale such as Basilosaurus. However, skeptics suggest the sightings are misidentifications of common animals such as otters, beavers, or lake sturgeon or inanimate objects such as floating logs.

GLOSSARY

annelids (A-neh-lidz) A family of creatures that includes earthworms, lugworms, and leeches.

Basilosaurus (ba-sil-oh-SAWR-us) A large marine mammal that lived between 56 and 35 million years ago. It had a long, slender body and very small limbs.

biologists (by-O-luh-jists) Scientists who study the natural world.

carcass (KAR-kus) The dead body of an animal.

cast (KAST) A three-dimensional shape, such as a footprint, made by shaping a material (such as plaster of paris) in a mold of that shape.

conger eel (KONG-ger EEL) A large eel that lives in shallow coastal waters.

corroded (kuh-ROHD-ed) Destroyed or damaged by chemical action.

cryptid (KRIP-tid) A creature that appears in stories, rumors, and legends, but whose existence is not recognized by science.

cryptozoologist (krip-tuh-zoh-O-luh-jist) A person who studies cryptids.

fur trapper (FUR TRA-per) A person who traps wild animals for their fur.

humanoid (HYOO-muh-noyd) Having an appearance resembling that of a human.

loch (LOK) A Scottish lake.

mammary glands (MA-muh-ree GLANDZ) The milk-producing glands of female mammals.

mirage (muh-RAHZH) An optical illusion caused by atmospheric conditions.

orangutan (uh-RANG-uh-tang) A large, mainly solitary tree-dwelling ape with long reddish hair, long arms, and hooked hands and feet, native to Borneo and Sumatra.

outhouse (OWT-hows) A small building, often used for storage, built close to but separate from a house.

phenomenon (fih-NO-muh-non) A fact or situation that is observed to exist or happen.

plaster of paris (PLAS-ter UV PA-rus) A soft, white substance made by the addition of water to powdered gypsum, which hardens when dried. It is used for making sculptures and casts.

plesiosaur (PLEE-see-uh-sawr) A large extinct marine reptile. It had a broad, flat body, large, paddlelike limbs, a long flexible neck, and small head.

rabies (RAY-beez) A contagious and fatal disease of dogs and other mammals. It causes madness and convulsions and can be transmitted to humans through the saliva.

serpentine (SUR-pen-teen) Winding and twisting like a snake.

Sherpa (SHERP-ah) A member of a Himalayan people living on the borders of Nepal and Tibet, renowned for their skill in mountaineering.

skink (SKINGK) A lizard with short limbs that typically burrows in sandy ground.

sonar (SOH-nahr) A system for detecting objects underwater by emitting sound pulses and measuring their return after being reflected.

sperm whale (SPERM HWAYL) A toothed whale with a massive head, which typically feeds at great depths on squid.

sturgeon (STUR-jen) A very large primitive fish with bony plates on the body.

toxin (TOK-sun) A poison from a plant or animal.

FURTHER READING

Godfrey, Linda. *Lake and Sea Monsters*. Philadelphia: Chelsea House Publishers, 2008.

Regan, Lisa and Chris McNab. *Urban Myths and Legendary Creatures*. Milwaukee, WI: Gareth Stevens Publishing, 2011.

Townsend, John. *Bigfoot and Other Mysterious Creatures*. New York: Crabtree, 2008.

Townsend, John. *Strange Creatures*. Mankato, MN: Smart Apple Media, 2009.

WEB SITES

Due to the changing nature of Internet links, PowerKids Press has developed an online list of Web sites related to the subject of this book. This site is updated regularly. Please use this link to access the list:

www.powerkidslinks.com/mysthunt/bigfoot/

INDEX